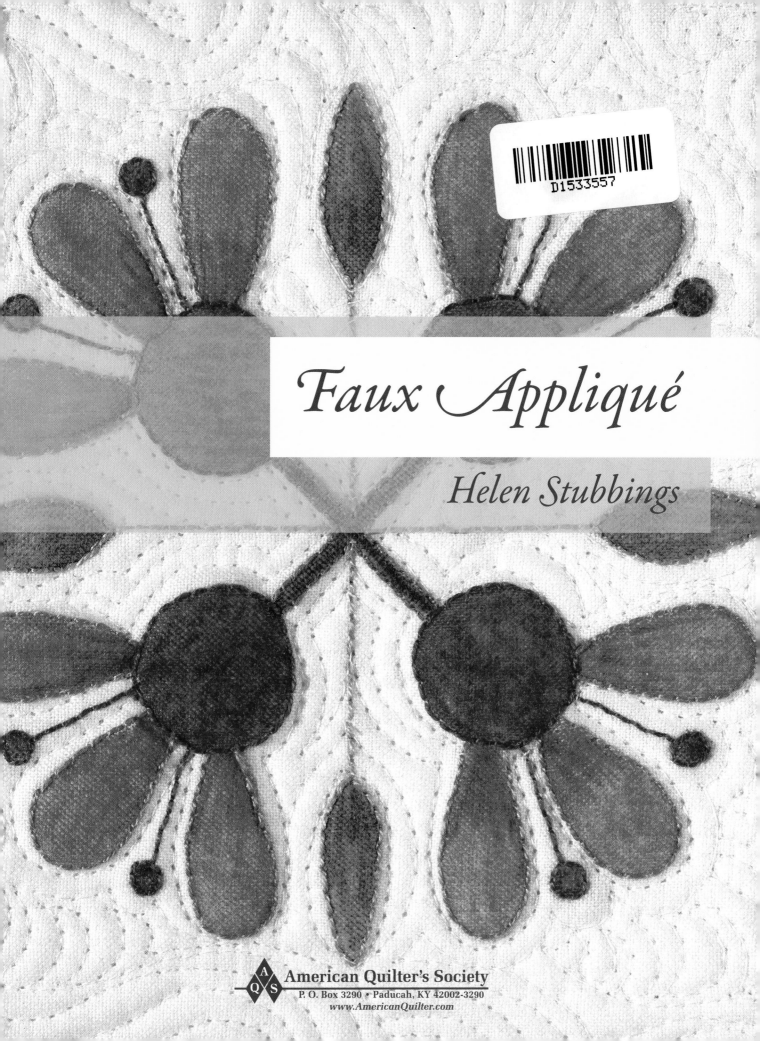

Faux Appliqué

Helen Stubbings

American Quilter's Society
P. O. Box 3290 • Paducah, KY 42002-3290
www.AmericanQuilter.com

Located in Paducah, Kentucky, the American Quilter's Society (AQS) is dedicated to promoting the accomplishments of today's quilters. Through its publications and events, AQS strives to honor today's quiltmakers and their work and to inspire future creativity and innovation in quiltmaking.

EXECUTIVE EDITOR: ANDI MILAM REYNOLDS
GRAPHIC DESIGN: ELAINE WILSON
COVER DESIGN: MICHAEL BUCKINGHAM
PROJECTS AND HOW-TO PHOTOGRAPHY: CHARLES R. LYNCH
GALLERY PHOTOGRAPHY: RICHARD BARREN
ADDITIONAL PHOTOGRAPHY: HELEN STUBBINGS

Additional copies of this book may be ordered from the American Quilter's Society, PO Box 3290, Paducah, KY 42002-3290, or online at www. AmericanQuilter.com.

Text © 2008, Author, Helen Stubbings
Artwork © 2008, American Quilter's Society

Library of Congress Cataloging-in-Publication Data

Stubbings, Helen.
    Faux appliqué / by Helen Stubbings.
        p. cm.
    ISBN 978-1-57432-971-1
    1. Quilting--Patterns. 2. Textile painting. I. Title.

TT835.S748 2008
746.46--dc22
                                    2008045429

American Quilter's Society
P. O. Box 3290 • Paducah, KY 42002-3290
www.AmericanQuilter.com

Proudly printed and bound in the United States of America

Dedication

With love to my chef, my cleaner,
my babysitter, my friend and my husband—
one and the same—for supporting my passion
and trying his very best to understand it......

A few thoughts on why we stitch:

It feels good to MAKE something with our own HANDS.

It feels good to know we CAN make something with our OWN hands.

It feels good when OTHERS comment on and COMPLIMENT us for our ACHIEVEMENTS.

It feels good when we GIVE something we make to others and see their REACTIONS.

It feels good to see something we make FINISHED and DISPLAYED or USED and ADORED.

IT FEELS GOOD.

Acknowledgements

By far and above all I wish to thank my sister, Tracey Browning. It was she who introduced me to the wide world of quilting.

TRACEY (LEFT) AND HELEN (RIGHT)

Although I first dabbled in patchwork and quilting as part of a needlecraft skills course I was completing, it was Tracey who showed me quilting's infinite limits.

She has encouraged my skills and business ventures, bounced and brainstormed ideas, listened to my concerns, instilled the confidence in me to take my techniques to the greater world, and inspired in me to do bigger and better things.

My appreciation of the quilting process hit like a gale force wind when we visited MQS (Machine Quilters Symposium) in 2006. This again opened my eyes to many more possibilities to explore, extend, and improve my skills.

And, of course I have to thank her for the exquisite work she does on her longarm machine with my quilts and projects. (She quilted most of the projects in this book on her A1 quilting machine.)

Our first exhibited combined quilt, DAISY DANCE, was shown across Australia and the USA, winning many awards for its quilting and design. BLESSED BALTIMORE has already been awarded several prizes in both countries, and our LACE #2 quilt won the Wall Machine Workmanship Award at Paducah in 2007.

I hope we can make many more beautiful things together. This book would not have happened without her.

I thank my parents daily for raising me with the skills to be resourceful, to use my hands in every way possible, and to use my brain and creative talents to create opportunities to share with the stitchers of the world.

To my husband and beautiful girls, not a day goes by that I do not appreciate how lucky I am. You are wonderful, and although you make sacrifices for my passion, I know that you are proud and supportive of all I do. My wish is that you, too, will experience the thrill of creating and stitching to bring joy to others. And that you live long and fulfilled lives achieving all of your dreams.

MY SUPPORT TEAM

To stitchers worldwide, thank you so much for your enthusiasm, your thirst for learning, and your caring and sharing nature. You keep me inspired to also learn and to create continually, soaking up information and using anything that comes my way to attempt and achieve new things both in stitching and in life...

Contents

Introduction

I first began adding color to my stitchery designs in 2001 to give depth and interest to the designs and to add an extra element of achievement to my work.

I began with paint. Craft paint was widely available; it was being used for folk art crafts and sometimes on fabric. However, I found that students and stitchers felt they had to be an 'artist' to use paint and they had to purchase special brushes and paints to do it.

Hence I thought, color pencils! We all colored in kindergarten! And so began my journey of playing, testing, experimenting, pushing the boundaries, and formalizing the Colourqué® technique.

What is Colourqué and how do I pronounce it?

Colourqué is simply using colored pencils on fabric to give an appliqué effect or appearance. Pronounced "Kulla-kay" in my Australian tongue or "Color-kay" in the States, it can replace needle turn, shadow trapunto, fused appliqué—even pieced appliqué.

Faux Appliqué — Helen Stubbings

How permanent is Colourqué?

While I have quilts that have been washed several times and I have tested patches—in many forms of detergent, hot and cold water, hot dryers, and hot sun for colorfastness, bleeding, and crocking—I believe that if you have put your heart and soul into a large project, to keep it looking at its best it should not be repeatedly laundered.

Like any fabric, dyed item, or clothing, a Colourquéd quilt will deteriorate and fade over time if washed weekly. The technique is designed for craft and art projects that are hung on a wall or laundered only when absolutely necessary. Treat your work as you would any needle-turned piece—with respect, love, and care.

A note on quilting

Although I am capable of some quite acceptable quilting on my domestic machine, my sister, Tracey Browning, is an expert quilter. We combine our talents regularly, each preferring to keep to our areas of expertise. I therefore have no hesitation on handing my designs over to her for her to finish with her exceptional workmanship and skills on her longarm quilting machine, as with the projects in this book. However, every project in this book may be quilted by domestic machine or by hand.

About this book

In this book I explain the basic form of Colourqué, which is user-friendly and fun to do! Plus, over the past few years, I have extended the technique using different pencils and different methods of stitching; I give you a peek at how you can go one step further with Colourqué later in the book.

Unless otherwise noted, the projects in this book are created in this order: color, seal, stitch. This process preserves the colors as you see them when the coloring is finished. Another process is to color, stitch, seal. This version makes the sealing easier as you have a boundary to work with, however, a lot of the intensity of color will be lost during the stitching process.

Color Pencils

We all have color pencils in the house somewhere and to get started it really doesn't matter what brand or type they are. I vividly remember saving my pocket money as a child to purchase my very own set of "special" pencils—Derwent artist pencils. They came in a pack of 24 in a plastic folder. I treasured those pencils and I still have them, albeit a little shorter today 30 years later! My children all love and treasure their pencils and are forever drawing and coloring something.

Products & Supplies

Pencils

Any color pencil can be used with this technique. However, the better the quality the pencil is, the softer the lead and the easier it is to transfer the color onto the fabric.

I use and recommend the Derwent ranges of pencils produced by the Cumberland Pencil company in the United Kingdom. These pencils are available worldwide; if I put a color name and number on a pattern, you can match it exactly. You may also use any other brand of pencil and choose similar or different colors for your projects.

Derwent pencils come in many ranges. The two I recommend and use for the basic version of the Colourqué technique are the Artist and Studio ranges. There are 72 colors in the Studio range. These pencils have a slim hexagonal barrel and a narrow, highly pigmented color strip for maximum color purity and fine detailed work. The Artists range has 120 colors and is a traditional, round wooden barreled pencil with a large diameter and a break-resistant color strip. These pencils are capable of both intense color and delicate shading. The color shades are the same, with the numbers being listed as two digits for Studio and four for Artists, i.e., 19, Madder Carmine (Studio) and 1900, Madder Carmine (Artists).

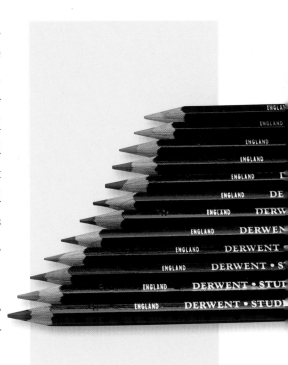

Derwent pencils also come in Colorsoft, Inktense, Watercolor, Pastel, and many other ranges. For this book we will stick to the Artist and Studio ranges and the basic form of Colourqué.

A pencil sharpener is an absolute must. See Care and Use on page 13 for detailed information.

Sealing medium

There are many brands and types of sealing mediums on the market. I have tested, use, and recommend the Folk Art® Textile Medium™ made by Plaid. It is available in 2oz, 4oz, and 8oz bottles and can be fairly easily found. There are details in the Resources section on page 94 if you don't know where to look. If you use other brands of textile medium, test them on a scrap first. Some are milkier and dull your color, and some are thicker and leave a shiny plastic feel to your fabric which is more difficult to stitch through.

Brushes

A small round paintbrush is all you need to apply the sealer. It does not have to be an expensive art brush but it does need to have natural or synthetic hair bristles, not the really cheap children's plastic type. If you wash it well and look after your brush it will last many years. A small flat brush is also handy for straight edges and filling larger spaces.

Stabilizers

To make it easier on your hands and wrists, I advise stabilizing your fabric while coloring. You can use freezer paper as found in quilt stores or supermarket shelves. You can buy it in rolls or in pre-prepared sheets designed for your inkjet printers. It is invaluable. A hot iron is used to fuse the shiny side to the back of your design fabric. It can be peeled off and reused many times. If it lifts during coloring, just refuse with your iron again. If it is not sticking well, your iron may not be hot enough or the freezer paper may be too old.

Alternatively, you can place your fabric onto fine grit sandpaper or Wet and Dry silicon carbide abrasive paper. A 600 grit or finer is recommended. This will grip your fabric and also act as an abrasive, which moves the color off the pencil and onto the fabric. These are readily available at your hardware store.

When coloring, ensure that you have a flat, smooth surface beneath your stabilizer and fabric or you will get colored texture on your design. It may be worthwhile making a "coloring board" by gluing your sheet of Wet and Dry or sandpaper to a plain piece of medium density fiberboard (MDF) plywood or smooth chipboard.

Fabrics

You can use the Colourqué technique on any fabric. Obviously for quilting type projects, 100 percent cotton fabric is preferred. For your coloring to show, it needs to be a light and fairly plain fabric. If using the Colourqué technique on patterns or darker shades, you will need to use contrasting pencil colors in dark shades for the images to be visible.

I like to use a tight weave with a high thread count so that the color does not need to be "pushed" into troughs and valleys between the fibers but can just sit on top. A quality quilter's muslin, PDF (prepared for dying fabric), homespun, sateen, or a fine linen will all work nicely for anything from wholecloth or large pieced quilts to tote bags and cushions. Tone on tones, marbles, hand-dyeds, or very small prints in neutral or very pastel colors will also work.

Faux Appliqué — Helen Stubbings

Fusible batting

I like to use a very lightweight fusible batting behind all of my stitcheries. This allows you to "jump" across from one point to another with your thread when stitching, hide knots or danglys, and also gives a lovely quilted look to your design. It means you can have fun with your stitching and not have to worry about perfect backs to your designs.

A non-fused batting can be used with a spray adhesive such as J. T. 505® Spray and Fix or a quilt basting spray, or you can just tack the batting to the fabric. One downside to using the fusible type is that it has little round glue dots and if you have to add more color after fusing, then you get little dots on your coloring. However the convenience and ease of fusing outweighs this problem in my opinion. Of course you do not have to use anything behind your stitching; this is just my preference.

Needles

The Colourqué technique calls for hand stitching the outlines of the motif designs. For hand outline or backstitching I like to use a size 7 or 8 crewel needle. These needles, sometimes referred to as embroidery needles, have a sharp point with a large eye for ease of threading and are medium in length, which makes them easy to handle for all ages, skill levels, and hand sizes. They can take up to 4 strands of a stranded (multi-ply) cotton thread with ease, or perle, crochet, and most specialty threads. They are available in sizes 1 to10.

It is important to select the right size needle for your fabric and thread. If the needle is too small, it will not make a large enough hole as it passes through the fabric, and your thread will become frayed and worn. If the needle is too large, you may have trouble stitching fine details and stitches on some fabrics, and it may leave holes in between stitches. As most of my stitching is done with only one or two strands of a stranded cotton thread or a fine perle type thread, the #7 or 8 needle is most useable.

Threads

The range of threads available on the market today is endless. For most of my patterns and books using the basic Colourqué technique, I have used a stranded cotton thread. These are types which come as a 6-ply skein of thread and are produced by DMC, Anchor, Presencia, and many more. The strands need to be separated first. Then lay the chosen number of strands together for smooth stitching.

We all have our favorite thread brands and any of them will work. The projects in this book use the Presencia® range of threads. They produce a Finca Perle cotton #16 thread that is packaged on a roll like a DMC® or Anchor® Perle thread and is equivalent to 1½ strands of a 6-ply cotton thread. Their range comes in several sized balls in 123 solid colors and 33 variegated colors. Finca Perle thread runs off the reel easily, is colorfast, has a smooth sheen, and eliminates the need for separating 6-ply threads. It could be substituted easily with one or two strands of a cotton thread or a lovely specialty thread for extra interest. I have listed equivalent DMC colors in the Resource section.

You may choose to use and experiment with any thread. As long as your needle size is correct and the thread size and type produce the results you want, then it will work. There is no right or wrong and there are no "thread police" watching!

Faux Appliqué — Helen Stubbings

Care and Use

Pencils

As with all pencils, you need to treat them with love and respect. The better the quality of the pencils you use, the softer the lead or graphite in them, which is what makes it easier to transfer the color onto your fabric. However, it is also easer to break the leads by dropping or mishandling your pencils. So keep them in their original tins or a protected case and take care not to drop or roughly handle them. If the lead shafts are broken by dropping, they will continue to break when you attempt to sharpen them.

Sharpeners

To use a pencil sharpener, keep the pencil and the sharpener in a straight line. Do not insert the pencil at an angle or the point will be subjected to unnecessary pressure and may break. Pencil sharpeners work very well when new and sharp, but do not last nearly as long as people think. There are a couple of easy ways to check whether a sharpener is blunt:

❑ Examine the wood around the pointed pencil. If the surface of the wood is smooth, then the sharpener is sharp. If the wood is rough or furry, then the sharpener is becoming blunt. A very blunt sharpener will produce a very rough surface on the pencil point.

❑ Watch the shavings coming out of the sharpener. A good pencil sharpener will produce a long, continuous sliver of shavings. The blunter the sharpener, the smaller the pieces of shaving become. If you start to see shard-like pieces coming out of the sharpener, then discard it.

Brushes

It is essential to thoroughly clean your brushes after each sealing session. The textile medium dries quite quickly and once dry on your brush is very difficult, if not impossible, to remove. Although you do not need expensive artists' brushes, it is still sensible to look after them to prolong their life.

Wipe off any excess medium from the bristles. Don't force the medium up into the ferrule (the hard part where the bristles meet the handle) of the brush. Gently wash in warm water and, if necessary, a small quantity of mild soap to remove all traces of medium. Rinse again in clean warm water. Gently shape the bristles into a nice round shape with your fingers and allow to dry at room temperature without resting the brush on its head. Always store brushes with their bristles upright.

Textile medium

Not much can go wrong with your textile medium. Just ensure that the lid is closed securely and keep at room temperature.

Needles

Always store your hand sewing needles in a natural fiber pin cushion or needlebook to prevent rusting. Needles are not expensive, so if one becomes bent or tarnished, please treat yourself to a new one. I use several needles at one time with a different thread color in each.

General Instructions

Mitered seams

Fold all your strips in half and lay them on a straight line on your cutting mat with the ends crossing the 45° line. Cut off all of the strip ends at the 45° angle (a).

Place two angled strip ends right sides together and stitch with a ¼" seam, taking care not to stretch the bias seam. You can see that the strips actually lie at right angles to each other (b).

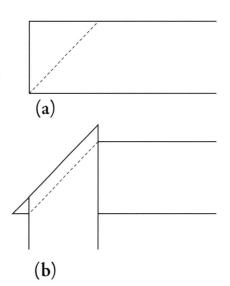

(a)

(b)

Hanging sleeve

Whether you're making a small or large wallhanging or quilt, it is always easier to attach a hanging sleeve before you bind your work.

Cut a strip of fabric approximately 9" wide and the same width as your finished quilt. Turn in a double ½" hem at both short ends and stitch it down, using a matching thread.

Press the strip in half wrong sides together and then open out again and sew a line of stitching ¼" from the folded crease on one side only, again using a matching thread.

Position the folded strip with raw edges even along the top of the back of your quilt with the row of stitching hidden against the quilt back. Baste. When you attach the binding to the front, you will secure the sleeve in that stitching line.

After hand stitching the binding to the back of your quilt, hand stitch the sleeve's lower edge. Pin the sleeve approximately 1" from the bottom edge to the quilt back (c).

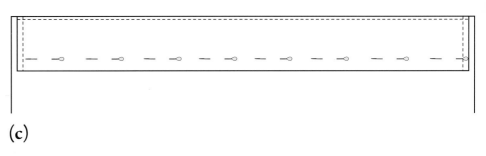

(c)

Lift the sleeve slightly to reveal the row of stitching you made earlier and use this line as a guide to hand stitch through the quilt backing layer only. This allows some "give" to the sleeve for a rod to pass through without distorting the front when hanging.

Mitered corners

Many years ago my sister, who was shown from someone else, who was shown from someone else, showed me this mitered corner technique, which I use on all of my bindings to get perfect corners without stitching after. While I cannot claim it as mine, I also cannot tell you its origin. However, whoever shared it with us I am sure would be happy to share it with you all.....

Use it on any bindings larger than ½" finished. A walking foot may make applying your binding easier and more accurate; otherwise a ¼" foot is recommended.

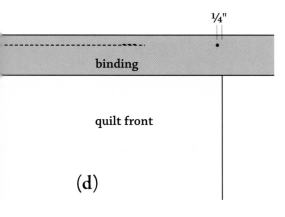

□ Beginning along one side and leaving a 10" tail, stitch your doubled binding strip to the right side of your quilt top using a ¼" seam. Stop sewing approximately 2" to 3" before the corner. Backstitch to secure and cut the thread.

(d)

□ Mark a dot ¼" from the corner with a pencil or permanent pen (on the binding strip) on the stitching line (d).

□ Using a ruler or square template, mark across the binding level with the first dot and then 90 degrees from it, forming a triangle. Fold the binding under itself from the corner dot (B) and stitch from A to B to C (e).

(e)

□ Trim off the corners and open out the binding strip. Continue your stitching line from where you previously finished 2" to 3" from the corner all the way to point A. Backstitch and cut the thread (f).

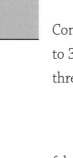

□ Turn the binding strip to the new direction. Fold any extra fabric aside and begin stitching from point A once again (g).

(f)

Faux Appliqué — Helen Stubbings

❒ Repeat for all four corners.

❒ Join the loose ends of your strips using a bias seam. (This is a bit fiddly but much nicer than a straight seam.) Stop on the last binding seam approximately 10" from your starting point.

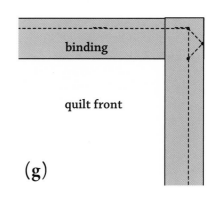

(g)

❒ Open out and lay both ends over the top of each other and mark a point on the raw edge where they meet. Mark another point ¼" longer than this point on each tail. Use your ruler and place the 45° line on the marked points and cut (h).

❒ Twist and lay each tail right sides together and stitch with a ¼" seam (i).

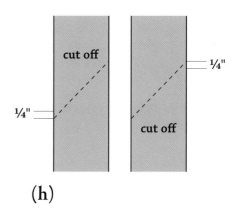

(h)

❒ Finger press open and reposition the joined binding strip along the quilt edge. Complete your stitching line.

❒ Once the binding is finished and turned, you will have a sewn mitered corner on both the front and the back.

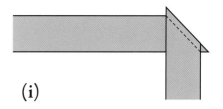

(i)

Other general tips

- ❏ Please read through all instructions carefully before beginning each project.
- ❏ All projects use the color, seal, then stitch method unless otherwise noted.
- ❏ I recommend that all fabric be 100 percent cotton quality patchwork fabric.
- ❏ Use 100 percent cotton thread for piecing.
- ❏ Requirements given are based on non-directional fabrics with a 40" useable width.
- ❏ Fabric allowances are generous to allow for prewashing, squaring, trimming, and minor slips of your ruler while cutting.
- ❏ Backing fabric yardage allows at least 4" around all edges of your quilt so that your bindings may be plump and healthy.
- ❏ The projects are easiest cut and most accurately made using a rotary blade cutter, ruler, and cutting mat. Templates may be made if you do not have this equipment.
- ❏ I recommend prewashing all fabric, checking for colorfastness, and pressing well.
- ❏ To cut strips, fold fabric selvedge to selvedge, then cut across the width, squaring the folded fabric every few strips for straightness.
- ❏ All seams are ¼" unless otherwise stated. Seam allowances are included in the sizes given in the cutting instructions.
- ❏ Fabrics are placed right sides together unless otherwise instructed.
- ❏ You will need a ¼" machine foot, walking foot, and sewing machine in good working order for optimal ease of and accuracy in sewing your quilts.
- ❏ Press all seams with a dry hot iron as directed.
- ❏ Use a walking foot when attaching bindings.
- ❏ Change your sewing machine needles regularly, perhaps every 3 bobbins' worth of thread. Regularly service your machine, keep it clean, and in good working condition. It is your best friend!

Faux Appliqué — Helen Stubbings

The Colourqué Technique

Some quilters may prefer to prewash their fabric before beginning. If you think it may shrink or bleed, I would recommend prewashing and pressing your background fabric.

For all projects in this book, I recommend prewashing your background fabric. The hand stitching will draw in your fabric blocks, so to prevent any further shrinkage, wash first.

I also recommend prewashing your red fabric in hot soapy water to test for colorfastness, as many red dyes can cause problems. You don't want to finish your quilt and have the red run into your beautiful stitched white blocks! Check that no running dye remains after washing by resoaking the red fabric in a tub of hot water.

You may also like to prewash your fusible lightweight batting in case of shrinkage. All battings react differently when washed, so to be sure, soak the batting in hot water and drape or hang to dry.

Transferring your designs

There are many ways to transfer designs from paper onto your background fabric. The method I find the easiest is using a light box or light source, such as a window or glass-topped table with a desk lamp underneath it, and a mechanical pencil.

First, tape your design sheet to the light source; then place your background fabric centrally over it. Tape each side to secure. Use the pencil to lightly trace all of the design elements onto the fabric, being careful not to stretch or move the fabric while tracing.

Faux Appliqué — Helen Stubbings

Stabilizing
Using freezer paper

Fuse the design to be colored onto a sheet of freezer paper: place the fabric wrong side down onto the waxy side of the paper and press with a hot iron until the wax has fused well to the fabric. Remember that any lumps and bumps on the fabric surface will show through on your coloring. A clean, smooth board or a thin stack of paper underneath your fused fabric can work if your table surface is rough.

Using fine grit paper

Lay your fabric onto the grit side of the sandpaper and place both on a smooth hard surface for coloring.

Coloring

Have your pencil colors chosen and sharpen the pencils, taking note of the sharpening hints on page 13 from the Cumberland Pencil Company.

When coloring, do not be afraid to add the color quite darkly. You can begin softer and build up layers to get darker color, or you can press quite hard from the start.

You need to color right to the drawn lines. Some people tend to fear going over them and leave a small white gap around the inside edge of their lines. Color right to the lines, even over the lines directly, but not outside them.

We were all taught in kindergarten not to go over the lines, and we have that bit right, but we were also told to color all in one direction. It is not so imperative here if you are using quality pencils.

Sometimes a circular movement works well and sometimes straight up and down is easier. It really depends on the shape you are coloring, the orientation of your work on the table, and the hue intensity you desire.

The goal is to have even coverage with no white or light spots throughout. In your base color you don't want to be able to see stroke lines, but if they are visible, just color another layer over the top until you have it even. Do whatever works best for you, and above all things, enjoy the process, don't stress!

(a)

Color right to the edges of your shape. Do not leave white lines between the color and the drawn shape (a). Color right on the line itself to ensure you haven't missed anything.

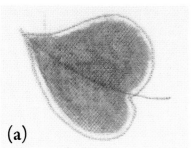

(b)

Color the shape evenly so that you don't get white or light spaces (b).

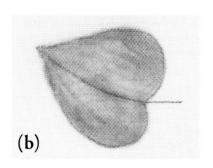

(c)

If you have white or light spaces as shown in the top side of this leaf, color another layer until you have even coverage across the whole shape, as shown on the bottom side (c).

Layering and even coloring will eliminate the pencil or stroke lines shown here (d). Use an even pressure across the shape in a circular motion or in a single direction to prevent stroke patterns.

(d)

When coloring with two colors, first color the entire shape with an even base of the lighter color. The darker shade is then used to add dimension or shape by feathering small light strokes from one side. Envision the light coming from one direction and add the shadow to the opposite side across the design.

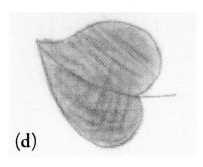

Faux Appliqué — Helen Stubbings

I don't worry too much about this, not being a trained artist, but instead I try to create shape and curves to things by giving a shaded edge to a leaf, for example. Colourqué is for everybody, not just artists, so we don't want to get bogged down with "coloring political correctness" here.

Some points on blending:

You don't want a definite line between two blocks of color. To prevent or correct a line:

- ❑ When using small feathery strokes from the outside edge inwards, you get a fine tip to your stroke and an uneven edge to the shaded area.
- ❑ Also, use different length strokes so that you do not create a straight edge of color.
- ❑ If your blending is too obvious, use the tip of your finger (body heat) and rub in a circular motion to move and blend the color.
- ❑ You can also improve the blending with the brush and medium at the sealing stage.

Some points on mistakes:

If you go over the line, if you don't like what you have colored, or if the color has rubbed onto your background fabric, DON'T PANIC!

- ❑ If you don't seal it, it won't stay there.
- ❑ You can use a normal clean white pencil eraser to try to remove the bulk of the color and recolor over it.
- ❑ You can wash the piece completely to remove the bulk of the color and recolor over it.
- ❑ You can leave the errant color to wear and rub off in time.
- ❑ You can use a toothbrush and some detergent to remove just a small portion of color.

(e)

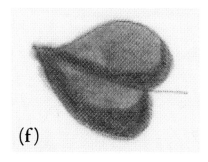

(f)

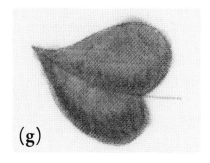

(g)

(h)

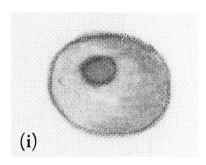

(i)

Bottom line: Any bits of color that crock or rub onto other parts of your fabric will wear off over time, as they won't be sealed, so don't worry about trying to remove them for now.

Feather light thin strokes from the outside edge (the right hand side in this case) towards the center. Use the most pressure at the edge and lift the pencil from the fabric as you feather towards the center to get a fine, uneven point. Make each stroke a different random length so an uneven feathery edge is gained (e).

Do not use even-length strokes or color in bands, as in (f). Blocks of color do not look realistic or attractive.

When all feathered strokes are of an even length, a blocked appearance still appears, as in (g). Keep the length random and uneven, as in (e).

Think of light coming from one direction as in the picture (e). Feather from one side only, as in leaf (e) and flower bud (i). This looks much more natural than from both sides as in (h).

Once you have finished all of your coloring you have a decision to make:

If you like your work exactly as it looks now, then you will take option one and seal it immediately, then stitch later.

However, if you feel that your coloring is too dark or too intense, or that your blending lines show up too much, or that your piece is not evenly colored, then you could choose option two. With option two you will outline stitch on all of your drawn lines first, and then seal the color. The process of stitching will take a lot of the color from the fabric. Just the movement of your hands over the fabric and the fabric rubbing onto itself will take a lot of the intensity out and blend any lines you may have. Also, the sealing process is now easier, as you have a stitched outline in which to seat your medium.

Faux Appliqué — Helen Stubbings

The option you choose is personal. I use both methods depending on the look I want and the colors used. If I have used very light color as in Daisy Dance (pictured on page 88), then I seal first or most of my color will disappear after stitching.

Plaid, the manufacturer of my textile medium brand of choice, recommends heat setting your coloring when using their medium with their paints on fabric. I have found this not to be necessary using the Colourqué technique, however, if you wish to do so, here are their instructions:

Heat Setting Your Fabric

Wait 24 hours after you have painted your project before heat setting. To make the paint adhere to the fibers and to make it more durable for washing, use a cloth that has been dampened with white vinegar—a piece of old sheet works great. Place the cloth over the painting. Then, using a dry setting on your iron, steam the vinegar-soaked cloth to set the paint.

If you use another brand of textile medium, follow their instructions.

Preparing for stitching

Once ready to stitch, I generally use a very lightweight fusible batting behind my design to stitch through. Cut a piece the same size as your fabric and lay the adhesive side up on an ironing board. Place your fabric wrong side down on the adhesive and fuse with a hot steam iron (or

following the manufacturer's directions) until the adhesive melts and holds to the fabric. I recommend placing your work in a 6"–8" embroidery hoop for stitching to give an even tension and neat appearance to your hand stitches. It also acts as an extra "hand" to hold your fabric taught for ease of stitching.

Stitching

In my basic version of Colourqué, all outline stitching is done by hand using a needle and thread. Most stitching uses only a small, even backstitch to cover all of the drawn lines. If you are really not into hand stitching, you can read about other methods of stitching the outlines in my gallery at the end of this book.

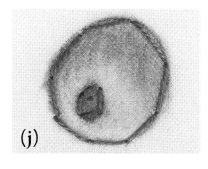

(j)

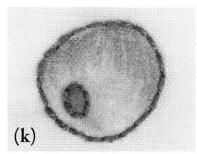

(k)

Choose your needle and thread. Insert your design into a small 6"–8" embroidery hoop and have it taut but not stretched out of shape.

Stitch over all the drawn lines using an even backstitch approximately ⅛" long. The stitch length depends on the size of your design. Larger designs may allow slightly larger stitch lengths if desired, but on smaller designs, you need a fine stitch length to get smooth, even curves.

Longer stitches produce a jagged, uneven curve (j); smaller stitches give a smooth, even curve (k).

Sealing

Here lies the beauty of pencil coloring: remember, if there are parts you don't like, if you went over the lines, or if the color has crocked or moved onto other parts of your fabric – DON'T SEAL IT – and it will wash out or eventually rub out.

Pour only the amount of textile medium you will use in one work session into a ceramic tile, paint palette, or small plastic bead container. (It will thicken and dry when exposed to the air.) I often use a lid from a plastic margarine container, which can be disposed of after use.

Use your small round paintbrush to paint the medium onto all of the colored areas you wish to keep. Do not push the medium onto the fabric, just lay it on top and let it soak in.

Do not get any onto the background fabric, as it will stain, and I have not found a way to remove this.

Move the medium close to the edges, ensuring you do not have too much on the brush at one time. This will cause it to bleed over the lines, taking color with it.

Faux Appliqué — Helen Stubbings

Practice on a scrap of fabric first to gauge how much and how close to the lines you need to go. It is really not difficult and you will soon get the hang of it.

You can use the brush to work your blending lines by pushing the medium into the color and moving the color around just like rubbing it with your finger. Just take care not to bleed the color outside of the lines.

You must ensure you cover all colored areas you wish to keep. If you leave small, empty spaces, the color will disappear through use or laundering and you will end up with light or white spots on your design. Ask me how I know this! I often miss a leaf or two when coloring a whole design and have to redo the coloring with difficulty after. So take heed and check that you have sealed every part of the design.

A caution on using dark colors: I have at times had trouble with dark colors, particularly reds, running after sealing. To prevent this or just for extra insurance, I like to *seal the front and back sides of any areas which have been darkly colored in red pigments.* I sometimes also seal the front again after stitching just to make sure I have taken all precautions. I don't want to finish a major project and have it ruined the first time it is laundered.

If in doubt when using a color or doing a major work, always test it first on a scrap of fabric.

Laundering

Once your quilt or project is finished it may be washed using your normal quilt laundering techniques.

Do not use bleach on Colourqué projects and do not leave them in full sun.

I would not recommend repeated laundering for a work of art, as like any cloth, textile, paint, or color finish, it may wear and fade over time.

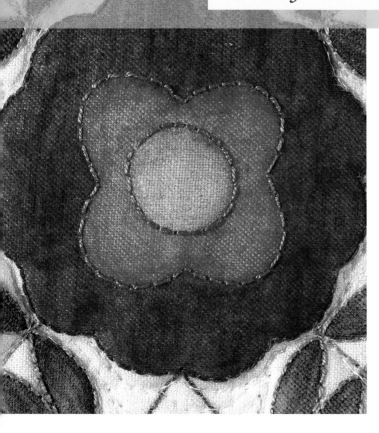

This palette was used for all of the projects in this book:

Pencils – Derwent Artist

1800 Rose Pink
1910 Claret
2100 Rose Madder Lake
5000 Cedar Green
5100 Olive Green

Presencia Finca Perle 16 Cotton

1996 Burgundy
2240 Rose Pink
4561 Grass Green
5229 Light Olive Green

Step-by-step instructions for coloring all of the projects:

Leaf 1

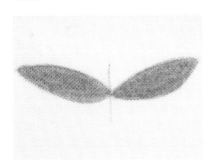

Color the complete shape with Color #5100, Olive Green.

Use light feathery strokes from both inner points outwards to give depth using Color #5000, Cedar Green.

Stitch the leaf outlines using 1 strand of Finca Perle 16 #5229, Light Olive Green.

Color the complete shape of Leaf 2 with Color #5100, Olive Green.

Use light feathery strokes from both points inwards to give depth using Color #5000, Cedar Green.

Color the complete shape with Color #1800, Rose Pink.

Blend the outside round edge lightly using Color #2100, Rose Madder Lake.

Stitch the leaf and stem outlines using 1 strand of Finca Perle 16 #5229, Light Olive. Stitch the bud outline using 1 strand of Finca Perle 16 #2240, Rose Pink.

Tip:

When sealing where you have used the very light pink, take care not to move any darker pencil colors onto the soft pink color. Seal the lightest areas first, making sure your brush is clean before beginning.

Leaf 3 (dark green stem and cup and flower bud)

Color the complete shape of Leaf 3 with Color #5000, Cedar Green.

Color the smaller half of the bud using Color #2100, Rose Madder Lake, and the larger half using Color #1910, Claret.

Stitch the green outlines using 1 strand of Finca Perle 16 #4561, Grass Green. Stitch the large half of the bud using 1 strand of Finca Perle 16 #1996, Burgundy, and the smaller half using 1 strand of Finca Perle 16 #2240, Rose Pink.

> **Tip:**
> Take care when sealing not to move the dark green color onto any of the pink areas. Paint all the green areas first, then clean the brush and proceed to the pink areas.

Bits and buds

Color the small circle buds of Bits and Buds using Color #1910, Claret.

Stitch the outlines of the small circle buds using Finca Perle 16 #1996, Burgundy. Stitch the curly stems using 1 strand of Finca Perle 16 #4561, Grass Green.

Faux Appliqué — Helen Stubbings

Flower 1 (large center flowers)

Color the center portion of Flower 1 using Color #1800, Rose Pink.

Color the middle portion using Color #2100, Rose Madder Lake.

Color the outer portion using Color #1910, Claret.

Blend the edges of the center portion lightly using Color #2100, Rose Madder Lake.

Blend the edges of the middle portion lightly using Color #1910, Claret.

Use 1 strand of Finca Perle 16 #2240, Rose Pink, to stitch the center and middle stitch lines. Use 1 strand of Finca Perle 16 #1996, Burgundy, to stitch the outside stitch line.

Tip:

When sealing where you have used the very light pink, take care not to move any darker pencil colors onto the soft pink color. Seal the lightest areas first, making sure your brush is clean before beginning.

Flower 2

Color the center portion of Flower 2 using Color #1910, Claret.

Color the middle portion using Color #1800, Rose Pink.

Color the outer portion using Color #2100, Rose Madder Lake.

Use 1 strand of Finca Perle 16 #2240, Rose Pink, to stitch the middle and outer stitch lines. Use 1 strand of Finca Perle 16 #1996, Burgundy, to stitch the center stitch line.

Faux Appliqué — Helen Stubbings

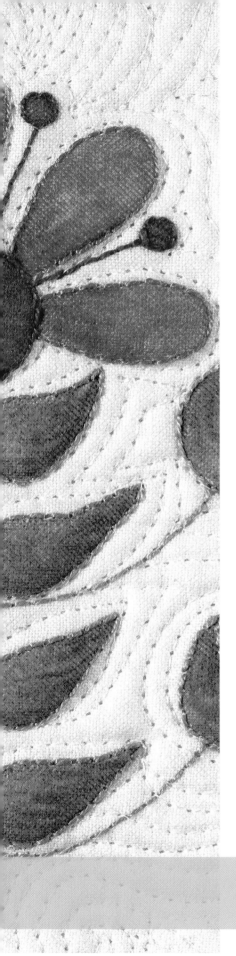

Flower 3

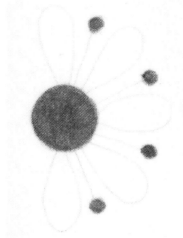

Color the center circle and small circle buds of Flower 3 using Color #1910, Claret.

Color the petals using Color #2100, Rose Madder Lake.

Blend the inner edges of the petals lightly using Color #1910, Claret.

Use 1 strand of Finca Perle 16 #2240, Rose Pink, to stitch the petals. Use 1 strand of Finca Perle 16 #1996, Burgundy, to stitch the center circle, the circle buds, and their stems.

Projects

Faux Appliqué — Helen Stubbings

16" x approx. 6½" diameter

Requirements

- ½ yd (40 cm) red fabric
- ½ yd (40 cm) plain light background fabric
- ½ yd (40 cm) fusible lightweight batting
- ½ yd (45 cm) batting
- ½ yd (45 cm) backing fabric
- 1½" (1½ m) yd piping cord
- ½ yd (½ m) thick red cord
- 16" (41 cm) square pillow form or bolster form

Cutting instructions

From white background fabric:
- Cut one piece 14" x 22"
- Three strips 3½" x leftover width

From red fabric cut:
- One strip 3½" x width of fabric
- Two strips 20½" x 5"
- Two strips 1½" x 24"

From fusible batting cut:
- One piece 14" x 22"

From interfacing cut:
- Two strips 2" x 20"

Colourqué

Copy the design onto paper. Attach this pattern to a light box or window light source.

Center the white background fabric on top of the design, with the design across the narrow width of the fabric as shown in the diagram (a).

Tape the pattern securely and trace it with a soft mechanical pencil.

Fuse the white 14" x 22" fabric to a sheet of freezer paper or use the fine grit sandpaper to stabilize it for your Colourqué step.

Colourqué the design following the General Instructions on pages 14–18 and the color guides given with each flower or leaf design.

Because dark reds can cause problems with bleeding, I suggest sealing both the front and back sides of the fabric now and again after stitching.

Fuse your large piece of fusible batting to the back of the Colourquéd fabric using a hot steam iron. Place the cooled piece in a 6"–8" embroidery hoop and stitch all of the lines following the photographs and thread color guides.

When you have finished all of your stitching, trim the block to measure 12½" x 20½". Center the design accurately before trimming the edges off.

Foundation-pieced border

Lay the 2 interfacing foundation strips over the 2" design pattern strips on page 86. Trace the triangles onto your foundation strips, moving the pattern strip along as you need to to fill in your fabric strip. You do not need corners on these strips, so begin your markings at the edge triangles only. Place an X where the red fabric goes (every other triangle) so you don't get mixed up as you piece.

From the 3½" strips of white and red fabric, rough cut 20 white and 20 red triangles using template A on page 87.

> **Tip:**
> Layer the red and white strips and cut 4–6 layers at once.

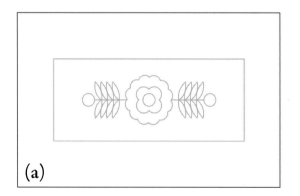

(a)

Follow your normal foundation piecing technique to piece the border strips.

Construction

Attach the foundation strips to either side of the Colourquéd panel. Remember to stitch along the interfacing edge to get perfect points.

Quilting

Lay the backing fabric on a flat surface. Smooth out any wrinkles. Lay the batting on top, again smoothing. Place your Colourquéd panel on top. You may wish to temporarily adhere or hand baste the layers together at this stage.

Quilt as desired or follow the photograph to mimic what we have done. All of the white background areas have been McTavished. Trim the backing and batting back to the edges of the panel.

Piping

Steam or prewash your piping cord to shrink it well.

Join your fabric strips and press the seams open. Press in half, wrong sides together, along the length.

Lay the cord inside the fold of the bias strip and push it right into the fold. Use a zipper, piping, or cording foot to stitch as close as possible to the cord without catching it. You may be able to adjust your needle position to perfect this.

Trim the edges of your piping ¼" from the stitching line as evenly as possible. Lay the piping strip raw edges even with the sides of your layered and quilted panel. Stitch on or to the left of the previous stitching line.

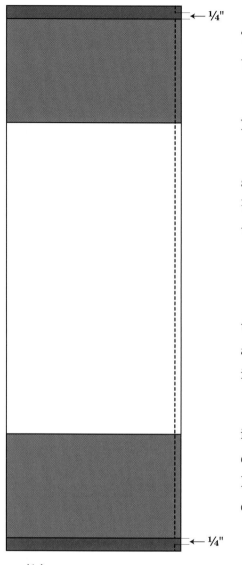

← ¼"

← ¼"

(b) *Double hem casing*

Pin a 20½" x 5" red strip of fabric over the top of your piping. Turn your work over and stitch through all of the layers exactly on top of the previous piping stitching line. Repeat on the other end.

Fold and press a ½" double hem on each end of the red fabric on your panel. Edge stitch using a matching thread.

Fold your panel in half wrong sides together. Match the piped seams and pin to hold in position. Stitch along the long edge with a ¼" seam allowance. Leave a ¼" opening at the beginning and end at the double hem to create a casing for the cord (b).

Trim any threads and turn through.

Use a safety pin to thread a piece of the red cord and feed it through the casing at each end. Gather the ends as tightly as possible and tie off securely at one end. Trim the ends of the cord and tuck inside.

Roll up your cushion insert/pillow form tightly into a tube and insert it into the bolster cover. (You may wish to roll and stitch it closed with a long straight stitch and strong thread for a good fit.) Pull up the cord tightly again and tie in a knot to secure. Trim the ends and tuck them inside the gathered opening.

Tip:

For perfect piping, I love the Groovin' Piping trimming tool and *Piping Hot Binding* book by Susan Cleveland. See the resource list, page 94, for details.

Faux Appliqué — Helen Stubbings

Colourqué pattern

BALTIMORE BOUNTY (*Square Pillow*)

16" x 16"

Requirements

¼ yd (20 cm) red fabric

½ yd (40 cm) plain light background fabric

½ yd (40 cm) fusible lightweight batting

½ yd (45 cm) batting

½ yd (45 cm) backing fabric

16" (41 cm x 41cm) square pillow form

15" (35 cm) zipper to match backing fabric

Cutting instructions

From white background fabric:

Cut one piece 15" x 15"

Four strips 3½" x leftover width

One piece 17" x 17" – quilt top backing

From red fabric cut:

Two strips 3½" x width of fabric

From fusible lightweight batting cut:

One piece 15" x 15"

From interfacing cut:

Two strips 2" x 12"

Two strips 2" x 16"

From pillow backing cut:

One piece 16½" x 14"

One piece 16½" x 5"

Colourqué

Copy the design onto paper. Attach this to a light box or window light source.

Center the white background fabric on top of the design, tape to hold, and trace with a soft mechanical pencil.

Fuse the traced fabric to a sheet of freezer paper to stabilize or use the fine grit sandpaper for your Colourqué step.

Colourqué the design following the General Instructions on pages 14–18 and the color guides given with each flower or leaf design.

Because dark reds can cause problems with bleeding, I suggest sealing both the front and back sides of the fabric now and again after stitching.

Fuse your large piece of fusible batting to the back using a hot steam iron. When cool, place your work in a 6"–8" embroidery hoop and stitch all of the lines following the photographs and thread color guides.

When you have finished all of your stitching, trim the block to measure 12½" x 12½". Center the design accurately before trimming the edges.

Foundation-pieced border

Lay the 2 shortest interfacing foundation strips over the 2" design pattern strips on page 86. Trace the triangles onto your foundation strips, moving the pattern strip along as you need to to fill in your fabric strip. You do not need corners on these strips, so begin your markings at the edge triangles only. Place an X where the red fabric goes (every other triangle) so you don't get mixed up as you piece.

Repeat with the two 16" strips, this time tracing the corner square onto both ends of each strip.

From the 3½" strips of white and red fabric, rough cut 28 white and 28 red triangles using template A on page 87.

Follow your normal foundation-piecing technique to piece the border strips.

> *Tip:*
> Layer the red and white strips and cut 4–6 layers at once.

Construction

Attach the 2 shorter foundation strips to either side of your Colourquéd panel. Remember to stitch along the interfacing edge to get perfect points. Press seams toward the pieced border strip.

Attach the remaining strips to the top and bottom of the panel, matching the corner seams carefully. Press towards the border strips.

Quilting

Lay out the pillow top backing, wrong side up, and smooth to remove any wrinkles, working on a large flat surface. Tape the backing to the table. Center the batting on top and smooth from the center outwards. Place the well-pressed pieced top on top of the batting and backing layers, and smooth out again.

Keeping the layers smooth at all times, pin or baste the pillow top ready for hand or machine quilting.

Quilt as desired or follow the photograph to mimic what we have done. All of the white background areas were filled with a McTavishing design. You could use any favorite filler here.

Pillow construction

To insert the zipper, place 2 backing pieces right sides together and lay the zipper centrally on top. Mark the beginning and end of the zipper. Using a ½" seam allowance, stitch with a normal stitch length from the edge to your first mark. Backtack to secure.

Now, using a long stitch length (the longest your machine will do), stitch to the next mark.

Return to a normal stitch length, backtack to secure, and stitch to the end. Press the seams open.

Lay the zipper on the wrong side centrally on the seam allowance being sure the zipper is right side down. Pin along its length. Using a zipper foot, stitch an even distance from the teeth down both sides using a normal stitch length.

From the front, use a seam ripper to remove the long basting stitches. Slightly open the zipper.

Lay the back wrong sides together with the quilted pillow top and sew around the outside edges. Trim the corners and any excess backing and turn the pillow through the zipper opening. Press well. Insert the pillow form; zip closed.

Note:
Remove the form if you need to launder the pillow top. Launder the top inside out.

Colourqué pattern

Faux Appliqué — Helen Stubbings

17" x 17" + Prairie Points

Requirements

½ yd (40 cm) red fabric

½ yd (40 cm) plain light background fabric

½ yd (40 cm) fusible lightweight batting

½ yd (45 cm) regular batting

½ yd (45 cm) backing fabric

Nine (9) 1" (2.5 cm) diameter red buttons

Cutting instructions

From white background fabric:

Cut one piece 15" x 15"

Two strips 1" x 14½"

Two strips 1" x 15½"

From red fabric cut:

Two strips 1½" x 12½"

Two strips 1½" x 14½"

Two strips 1½" x 15½"

Two strips 1½" x 17½"

Three squares 6½" x 6½"

Two template C (page 87) – trace around template, cut out leaving approximately ¼" seam allowance.

From fusible batting cut:

One piece 15" x 15"

Faux Appliqué — Helen Stubbings

Colourqué

Copy the design onto paper. Attach this to a light box or window light source.

Center the white background fabric on top of the design, tape to hold, and trace with a soft mechanical pencil.

Fuse the traced fabric to a sheet of freezer paper to stabilize or use the fine grit sandpaper for your Colourqué step.

Colourqué the design following the General Instructions on pages 14–18 and the color guides given with each flower or leaf design. The basket is colored in 1800, Rose Pink, with darker shading colored in 2100, Rose Madder Lake. It is stitched using Finca Thread 2240, Rose Pink.

Because dark reds can cause problems with bleeding, I suggest sealing both front and back sides of the fabric now and again after stitching.

Fuse your large piece of fusible batting to the back using a hot steam iron. When cool, place your work in a 6"–8" embroidery hoop and stitch all of the lines following the photographs and thread color guides.

When you have finished all of your stitching, trim the block to measure 12½" x 12½". Center the design accurately before trimming the edges.

Construction

After attaching each strip, press all seams to red.

- ❏ Attach a 12½" red strip to the top and bottom of your stitchery panel.
- ❏ Attach a 14½" red strip to the sides.
- ❏ Attach 14½" white strips to the top and bottom.
- ❏ Attach a 15½" white strip to the sides.
- ❏ Attach a 15½" red strip to the top and bottom.
- ❏ Attach a 17½" red strip to the sides.

Fold each 6½" square in half twice diagonally to make a prairie point. Press with steam.

Hanging tabs

Fold each template C piece in half, right sides together. Stitch around all of the outside edges on the drawn line. Make a small slit in the center of one layer only. Clip the corners and turn the tab through this opening. Fold the diamonds in half to make a triangle shape with the slit on the inside. Press with steam. You will have two hanging tabs. Set them aside.

Quilting

I have sewn my wallhanging pillowcase style, i.e., I constructed it right sides together with an opening left for turning it inside out, then seamed that opening closed, and then quilted it. I therefore have not used any binding.

To make your wallhanging the same way, first position your 3 prairie points with raw edges even along the bottom edge of your pieced top. Leave ¼" at either side of each point so none are caught in the side seams. Pin and baste into position.

Lay the batting on a flat surface. Lay the well-pressed backing fabric wrong side down on top and smooth out carefully. Place the hanging side right side down on the backing and smooth out any wrinkles. Pin all of the outside edges. Stitch a ¼" around the outside edges of the top, leaving a 3" opening on the bottom edge behind the prairie points (a).

Once the stitching is finished, trim all batting and backing to ¼" from the stitch line. Trim the corners and turn the hanging to the right side through the opening. Slip stitch the opening closed with a matching thread. Press well.

You can now do a little quilting if you wish. Tracey and I McTavished the white areas of the wallhanging.

Position the hanging tabs you set aside evenly along the top of your wallhanging. Secure them with a button at the point of each tab through all layers. Add a button to the top and bottom of each prairie point for effect.

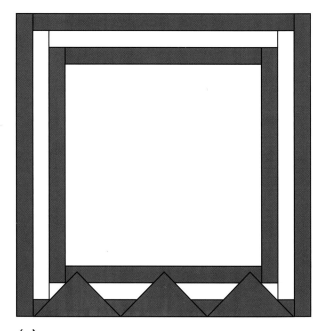

(**a**) *Pin the prairie points so they are not caught in the side seams.*

Colourqué pattern

MINI BALTIMORE *(Mini Quilt)*, 17" x 17"

Made by the author, quilted by Tracey Browning.

Faux Appliqué — Helen Stubbings

MINI BALTIMORE (*Mini Quilt*)

17" x 17"

Requirements *(see * under Quilting on page 53)*
⅓ yd (30 cm) red fabric
½ yd (45 cm) plain muslin background fabric
½ yd (45 cm) fusible lightweight batting
½ yd (45 cm) batting
½ yd (45 cm) backing fabric

Cutting instructions
From white background fabric:
Cut one square 18" x 18"
Four strips 2" x width of fabric

From red fabric cut:
4 strips 2" x width of fabric
2 strips 1½" x width of fabric (binding)

From fusible batting cut:
One square 18" x 18"

From nonfusible lightweight interfacing cut:
Two strips 1" x 15"
Two strips 1" x 17"

Center blocks – *use the nine full size blocks, pages 75–83, from your Baltimore quilt and copy them at 60% on a copier.*

Use a blue water-erasable pen to mark a 15" square onto the large plain background square. Mark nine equal parts by drawing a line at the 5" and 10" points in both directions (a).

Attach each design to a light box or light window source. Center each section of the marked square over the applicable design sheet (follow the photograph for placement) and secure with tape. Trace the design with a soft mechanical pencil.

Fuse the fabric to a sheet of freezer paper to stabilize or use the fine grit sandpaper for your Colourqué step.

Colourqué blocks following the General Instructions on pages 14–18 and the color guides given with each design.

Because dark reds can cause problems with bleeding, I suggest sealing both front and back sides of the fabric now and again after stitching.

Fuse the piece of lightweight batting to the back of your work using a hot steam iron. When cool, place your top in a 6"–8" embroidery hoop and stitch all of the lines following the photographs and thread color guides.

When you have finished all of your stitching, trim the block to measure 15½" x 15½". Center the design accurately.

Foundation-pieced border

Lay the 2 shortest interfacing strips over the 1" design sheet and trace the triangles using a soft mechanical pencil. Move the pattern strip along as you need to fill in the fabric strip. You do not need the corner triangles on these strips. Place an X where the red fabric goes so you don't get mixed up later.

Repeat with the two 17" strips, this time tracing the corner square onto both ends of each strip.

(**a**) *Center squares layout diagram*

From the 2" strips of white and red fabric, rough cut 60 white and 60 red triangles using template B on page 87.

> **Tip:**
> Layer the red and white strips and cut 4–6 layers at once.

Follow your normal foundation-piecing technique to piece the border strips.

Attach these 2 strips to either side of your center Baltimore panel. The stitching line should run along the edge of your interfacing strip, giving you perfect points. Press the seam towards the pieced border.

Attach the top and bottom strips in the same manner, ensuring you pin match your corners carefully.

Quilting

First check to see if your quilt is square. If not, it may need to be blocked.

Once the top is dry, lay out the backing, wrong side up, and smooth to remove any wrinkles, working on a large flat surface. Tape the backing to the surface. Center the batting on top and smooth from the center outwards. Place the well-pressed, pieced top on top of the batting and backing layers, and smooth out again.

Keeping the layers smooth at all times, pin- or thread-baste the quilt in a grid pattern starting from the center and working towards the edges at 4" intervals for hand or machine quilting.

*If your quilt will be machine quilted by a professional machine quilter, do not baste the layers. Allow an extra 3"–4" all the way around your quilt top, backing, and batting. Please refer to your own machine quilter's requirements.

Quilt as desired or follow the photograph to mimic what we have done. A motif was placed into each corner of the center block and then all backgrounds were filled with a McTavishing design. You could use any favorite filler here, but try not to take the spotlight away from the Colourquéd Baltimore designs with overpowering quilting. Because this is a miniature, any quilting you do needs to be balanced with and in proportion to the reduced size of the design.

Binding

Join the 2 strips of 1½" wide red binding fabric together using a 45° angle. Press the long strip in half, with the wrong sides together. Align the raw edge of the binding to the raw edge of the quilt top and sew with a ¼" seam, mitering the corners as you go. Trim the excess off the edges of the batting and backing to ⅛" from the seam line and turn the binding to the back.

To finish the quilt, slip stitch the binding to the back with a thread that matches the binding fabric.

Labeling

Last, but most important, make a label for your quilt that includes your name, address, the date, the name of the quilt, and any other relevant details. The best thing to use is a permanent pen to ensure the details don't wash away. Or, you may wish to make a Colourquéd label using a design feature from the front and embroider or pen stitch the writing with a permanent pen. Stitch this label to the back of your quilt for prosperity.

> *Tip:*
> If you attach the label before the quilting step, it will be quilted to the quilt and very difficult for another "lover" of your quilt to remove.

Helen Stubbings — Faux Appliqué

12" x 58"

Requirements

    ½ yd (40 cm) red fabric

    1 yd (75 cm) plain background fabric

    ⅔ yd (55 cm) fusible lightweight batting

    ½ yd (40 cm) batting

    ½ yd (40 cm) backing fabric

    Two (2) red tassels

Cutting instructions

From white background fabric:

    Cut one piece 10" x 35"

    Three strips 3½" x width of fabric

    2 strips 12½" x 2½"

    2 strips 12½" x 1"

    2 strips 6½" x 10" approximately

From red fabric cut:

    Three strips 3½" x width of fabric

    Four strips 12½" x 1½"

    2 strips 3½" x 6" approximately

    Three strips 2½" x width for binding (If you pillowcase your runner you will not need these strips. Read below before cutting.)

From fusible batting cut:

    One piece 10" x 35"

From non-fusible lightweight interfacing cut:

    Two strips 2" x 32"

Colourqué

Copy the main table runner design onto paper. Attach this to a light box or window light source.

Fold the white strip in half and finger press the center point. Lay this on the dashed center line of your design, ensuring it is centered on the width of your fabric. Tape it and trace the design with a soft mechanical pencil. Trace the end portion of the design (page 60) also.

Turn the strip around, again lining up the center line and trace the opposite end as before.

Fuse the fabric to a sheet of freezer paper or use fine grit sandpaper to stabilize it for the Colourqué step.

Colourqué the design following the General Instructions on pages 14–18 and the color guides given with each flower or leaf design.

Because dark reds can cause problems with bleeding, I suggest sealing both front and back sides of the fabric now and again after stitching.

Fuse the large piece of batting to the back of your work using a hot steam iron. When cool, place it in a 6"–8" embroidery hoop and stitch all of the lines following the photographs and thread color guides.

When you have finished all of your stitching, trim the block to measure 8½" x 32½", centering the design accurately along the length and the width of the fabric.

Foundation-pieced border

Lay the 2 shortest interfacing strips over the 2" design sheet and trace the triangles using a soft mechanical pencil. Move the pattern strip along as you need to fill in the fabric strip. You do not need the corner triangles on these strips. Place an X where the "red" fabric goes so you don't get mixed up later.

From the 3½" strips of white and red fabric, rough-cut 32 white and 32 red triangles using template A on page 87.

Tip:
Layer the red and white strips and cut 4–6 layers at once.

Follow your normal foundation-piecing technique to piece the border strips.

Construction

Attach the 2 foundation-pieced strips to either side of your center runner panel with the white edge to the center. The stitching line should run along the edge of your interfacing strip giving you perfect points. Press the seam towards the pieced border.

Lay your ruler from the ¼" mark at each end to the point, draw a line, and trim along the line, removing the excess. Repeat for the other end.

Place the center runner design (page 61) onto your light box or light source. Place the pieced runner end triangle unit on top with the seam line between the red strip and large white strip of the triangle on the dashed center line of the design. Tape to secure the fabric and trace the design as before with a soft mechanical pencil. Repeat for the other triangle end.

Colourqué the end units following the process noted above for this project and fuse both triangle end pieces to the remaining piece of fusible batting. Place your work in a hoop and complete all of the stitching.

Trim any batting from the edges and attach the triangles to each end of the table runner center. Press well.

For the runner's ends, attach the white and red strips in the following order (a):

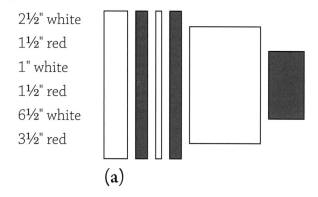

2½" white
1½" red
1" white
1½" red
6½" white
3½" red

(a)

As the strips get shorter, center them along the previous strip. This just needs to be approximate.

Press all seams towards the red fabric.

Fold the pieced end strip in half and finger crease the center point at the red end.

Mark ¼" from the left end with a pencil dot and at the center of your crease point at the right end (b).

(b)

Faux Appliqué — Helen Stubbings

Quilting

Lay out the backing, wrong side up, and smooth to remove any wrinkles, working on a large flat surface. Tape the backing to the surface. Center the batting on top and smooth from the center outwards. Place the well-pressed pieced top on top of the batting and backing layers, and smooth out again.

Keeping the layers smooth at all times, pin- or hand-baste the quilt in a grid pattern starting from the center and working towards the edges at 4" intervals for hand or machine quilting. Or, this being a small project, you may choose to spray baste the layers. Follow manufacturer directions.

Quilt as desired or follow the photograph to mimic what Tracey did, which was to fill all white background areas with a McTavishing design and stitch in the ditch between the strips at either end. You could use any favorite filler here, but keep it in the background so as not to take the spotlight away from your Colourquéd Baltimore designs.

Alternatively you may decide to pillowcase the runner and do light or no quilting. To do this, lay the batting on a flat surface. Lay the well-pressed backing fabric wrong side down on top of the batting and smooth out carefully. Place the runner top right side down on top of the backing and again smooth any wrinkles out.

Pin all of the outside edges or hand baste. Stitch ¼" around the outside edges of the top, leaving a 3" opening on one side. Remember to follow the edge of your interfacing strips to get perfect points.

Once you have finished stitching, trim the batting and backing to ¼" from the stitch line. Trim the points at each end and turn the runner to the right side through the opening. Slip stitch the opening closed with a matching thread. Press well.

You can still do a little quilting if necessary or desired. This pillowcase method eliminates the binding process below.

Binding

Join the 3 strips of 2½" wide red binding fabric together using a 45° angle. Press the long strip in half with the wrong sides together. Align the raw edge of the binding to the raw edge of the quilted runner top and sew with a ¼" seam, mitering the corners as you go. Trim the excess off the edges of the batting and backing to ½" from the seam line and turn the binding to the back.

To finish the table runner, slipstitch the binding to the back with a thread that matches the binding fabric.

Colourqué pattern

Faux Appliqué — Helen Stubbings

Colourqué pattern

Center line

**Use half-motif
for the end design.**

SIMPLY BLESSED *(Small Quilt)*, 40" x 40"
Made and quilted by the author.

Faux Appliqué — Helen Stubbings

40" x 40"

Requirements

⅓ yd (25 cm) mottled tan background fabric

1 yd (90 cm) various pink fabrics

¾ yd (70 cm) various green fabrics

1⅓ yd (1.2 m) batting

1⅓ yd (1.2 m) backing fabric
    (48"/120 cm wide)

⅓ yd (25 cm) dark red fabric for binding

Cutting instructions

From tan background fabric:

Cut 12 squares 4½" x 4½"

From various pink fabrics cut:

13 squares 4½" x 4½"

24 pieces 4½" x 2½"

24 pieces 8½" x 2½"

From various green fabrics cut:

26 pieces 4½" x 2½"

26 pieces 8½" x 2½"

From dark red binding fabric cut:

Four strips 2½" x width

Because dark reds can cause problems with bleeding, I suggest sealing both front and back sides of the fabric now and again after stitching.

Place in a 3"–4" embroidery hoop and stitch all lines following the photographs and thread color guides.

Colourqué

Copy the design onto plain paper. Attach this to a light box or window light source.

Center the tan background squares on top of the design, with the edges lined up with the outside square (a).

Construction

Attach a 4½" x 2½" pink strip to the top and bottom of each tan square.

Press seams towards the pink strips. Attach a 2½" x 8½" pink strip to both sides. Use the same fabric on the top and bottom and the sides of each square. Press seams towards the pink strips (b).

(a)

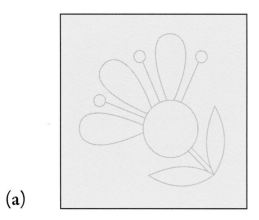

Tape the fabric to hold and trace the design onto it with a soft mechanical pencil. Fuse the fabric to a sheet of freezer paper or use the fine grit sandpaper to stabilize it for your Colourqué step.

Colourqué the design following the General Instructions on pages 14–18 and the color guides given with each flower or leaf design.

(b)

Ensure that the Colourquéd design is facing the same direction in every block; the quilt design is a directional one.

Faux Appliqué — Helen Stubbings

Attach a 4½" x 2½" green strip to the top and bottom of each pink 4½" square. Press seams to the green strip. Attach matching strips to both sides, and press seams to the green strip once more.

Lay out your blocks following the photograph in a pleasing and balanced manner. Turn the green-bordered blocks once clockwise so that there is a seamless edge butting against a pink-bordered block with a seam (c).

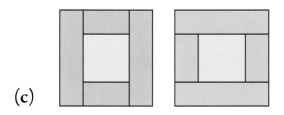

(c)

Join your blocks into 5 rows of 5 blocks each. Press all seams towards the green blocks.

Join the rows, matching all seam lines. If you pressed correctly as you assembled the pink- and green-bordered blocks, then the seam junctions will be mirrored and assist with perfectly matching them.

Lay the backing fabric on a flat surface. Smooth out any wrinkles. Tape or pin the backing to keep it smooth but not stretched. Lay the batting on top, smoothing it, also. Place your quilt top down and smooth well. Baste the layers together in the manner of your choice for machine or hand quilting.

Quilting

Quilt as desired or as I have done. Using an invisible polyester thread, I quilted in the ditch in the following pattern:

❏ First, use a walking foot and stitch the straight rows vertically, as shown in pink.

❏ Change to your free-machine foot and stitch a flower design in the center of each green block. You could make yourself a template for this and mark your blocks before quilting.

❏ Finally, I free-motion machine quilted down each seam in both directions. To avoid having to turn the quilt and having the least amount of quilt in your machine bed, stitch down each row (shown in aqua), then stitch backwards back up the other side of your seam (shown in green). Once you have completed every seam in the vertical position, you need to turn the quilt and do every horizontal seam in the same manner.

Binding

Join the 4 strips of 2½" wide red binding fabric together using a 45° angle. (See page 15 for instructions on mitered angles if you need them.)

Press the long strip in half with the wrong sides together. Align the raw edge of the binding to the raw edge of the quilt and sew with a ¼" seam, mitering the corners as you go. Trim the excess from the edges of the batting and backing to ½" from the seam line and turn the binding to the back.

To finish the quilt, slip stitch the binding to the back with a thread that matches the binding fabric.

Hanging sleeve

If your quilt will be entered into a competition, exhibition, or in your home, it is a good idea to attach a hanging sleeve as you attach your binding. See page 15 on hanging sleeve instructions if you wish to do this. If your quilt's future is to be a lap quilt, you will not need to attach a sleeve.

Labeling

Last, but most important, make a label for your quilt that includes your name, address, the date, the name of the quilt, and any other relevant details. The best thing to use is a permanent pen to ensure the details don't wash away. Or, you may wish to make a Colourquéd label using a design feature from the front and embroider or pen stitch the writing with a permanent pen. Stitch this label to the back of your quilt for prosperity.

Tip:
If you attach the label before the quilting step, it will be quilted to the quilt and very difficult for another "lover" of your quilt to remove.

Colourqué pattern

Faux Appliqué — Helen Stubbings

BLESSED BALTIMORE *(Cover Quilt)*, 54" x 54". *Made by the author, quilted by Tracey Browning.*

Faux Appliqué — Helen Stubbings

54" x 54"

Requirements

1¼ yd (1 m) red fabric

4yds (3.2 m) white background fabric

2½ yd (2.2 m) fusible lightweight batting

60" (1.5 m) batting

60" (1.5 m) backing fabric (60" wide) or

120" (3 m) backing fabric (40" wide)

Cutting instructions

From white background fabric:

Cut 9 squares 12" x 12"

Four strips 10" x 52"

13 strips 3" x width of fabric

From red fabric cut:

13 strips 3" x width of fabric

6 strips 2½" x width of fabric

From fusible batting cut:

Nine squares 12" x 12"

Four strips 10" x 52"

From nonfusible lightweight interfacing cut:

Two strips 2" x 30"

Two strips 2" x 34"

Two strips 2" x 50"

Two strips 2" x 54"

Colourqué the blocks following the General Instructions on pages 14–18 and the color guides given with each design.

Because dark reds can cause problems with bleeding, I suggest sealing both front and back sides of the fabric in each block now and again after stitching.

Fuse a piece of batting to the Colourquéd back using a hot steam iron. When cool, place the block in a 6"–8" embroidery hoop and stitch all of the lines following the photographs and thread color guides.

When you have finished all 9 blocks, press and trim each to measure 10½" x 10½", centering the designs on the blocks accurately.

Lay out the 9 squares following the photograph or according to your fancy and join them in 3 rows of 3. Press all seams open carefully from the back, taking care not to scorch the fusible batting. Pin-match the seams and join the 3 rows together.

Center blocks

Copy or trace each block design on the following pages onto a single sheet of paper. Attach each paper design to a light box or window light source.

Center a white fabric square over the design and secure with tape. Trace the design with a soft mechanical pencil.

Fuse the fabric to a sheet of freezer paper or use fine grit sandpaper to stabilize the fabric as you Colourqué.

Foundation-pieced inside border

Lay the 2 shortest interfacing strips over the 2" triangle foundation piecing design sheet on page 86 and trace, using a soft mechanical pencil. Move the fabric strip along as you need to to fill it in. Place an X where the red fabric goes so you don't get mixed up later.

Repeat with the two 24" strips, this time tracing the corner square onto both ends of each strip.

Faux Appliqué — Helen Stubbings

From the 3" strips of white and red fabric, rough cut 60 white and 60 red triangles using template A on page 87.

Tip:

Layer the red and white strips and cut 4–6 layers at once.

Follow your normal foundation-piecing technique to piece the border strips. Press well. Trim the strip to ¼" from all the edges of your interfacing.

Attach these 2 strips to either side of your center Baltimore panel. The stitching line should run along the edge of your interfacing strip giving you perfect points. Press the seam towards the pieced border.

Now attach the top and bottom in the same manner, ensuring you pin-match the corners carefully.

Colourqué border

Copy or trace the border design onto a single sheet of paper. Tape the paper design to your light box or window light source.

Fold each 52" white strip in half and finger press the center point. Line this up with the center point of the border design on the light box, secure it with tape, and trace the design softly with your mechanical pencil.

Now move the fabric strip and repeat the design once to the right and once to the left. Repeat with all 4 strips.

Following the Colourqué instructions used before, color and seal each border strip. Attach fusible batting to the back of each strip, *but only fuse to where the colored design finishes.* You will have approx 10" at each end of the strip where the fabric and batting are separated. Hand stitch all of your outlines as before, following the thread color guide.

When you have finished all of the stitching, trim the strips to 52" x 8½", ensuring you have the design centered equally along each strip.

Check-measure through the center of your quilt top. It should measure 34½". Fold and mark the center point of each border strip. Measure 17¼" in each direction and mark this point on the inside edge. See diagram (a).

Place the 45° line of your cutting ruler at this 17¼" mark and cut to the outside edge. Trim the batting back ¼" shorter than the fabric. Fold the batting back and pin it out of the way so that it doesn't get caught in any seams when you attach the border strips (a).

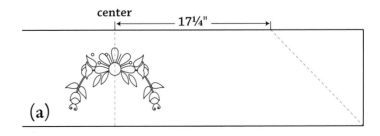

(a)

Prepare to attach each border to your quilt top by folding the top and the border in half and half again. Mark each fold point with a pin (¼ of the length, ½ of the length, ¾ of the length) and match the pins when you place the border strip on to the top. Pin the borders to the top.

Stitch the borders to the top, beginning ¼" from the beginning and end ¼" from the end. See diagram (b). Press seams outwards.

Now, fold the quilt right sides together diagonally and align the edges of the mitered corners at one corner of the quilt top. Stitch from the ¼" mark (where your previous two stitch lines started and ended) *from the inner seam to the outside edge.* Press the seams open, ensuring you don't fuse that batting down yet. Repeat for all of the corners.

Use the light box and the corner design sheet to lightly trace the 4 corner designs. Colourqué them following previous directions. Now fuse the batting in place. It should meet neatly at the mitered stitch line. Hand stitch all the corner designs as before.

Foundation-pieced outside border

Using the remaining strips of interfacing, lay them over the 2" outer border foundation-piecing design sheet and trace, using a soft mechanical pencil. Move the strip along as you need to to fill in the fabric. Mark the corner square onto both ends of both longer strips. Place an X where the red fabric goes to guide you as you piece.

From the 3" strips of both white and red fabric, rough cut 104 white and 104 red triangles using template A on page 87.

As with the inside foundation-pieced border, piece your strips and attach to the outer edges of your quilt.

Backing

If using a narrow backing fabric, cut it into 2 equal lengths 60" (1.5 m) long by the width of the fabric. Trim off the selvages and join the pieces side by side. Press the seam well. If using a wide backing cut to size, trim off the selvages and press well.

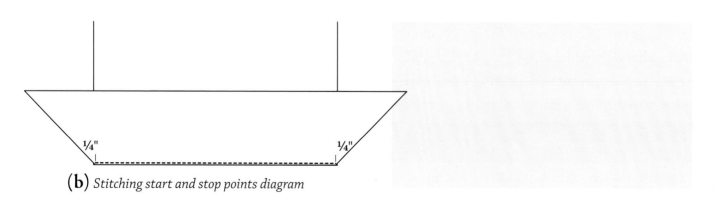

(b) *Stitching start and stop points diagram*

Faux Appliqué — Helen Stubbings

Quilting

Before layering, do one final check of the back side of your completed top. You are looking for any red threads, shadowing of red fabric, untrimmed seams, etc., that may show through the white fabric on the front when you are finished. You don't want to have basted it or even quilted it and then see one red thread lying between the layers which will forever haunt you!

Also check to see if your quilt top is square and block it if necessary.

Lay out the backing, wrong side up, and smooth to remove any wrinkles, working on a large flat surface. Tape the backing to the surface (an uncarpeted floor works well). Center the batting on top and smooth from the center outwards. Place the well-pressed pieced top on top of the batting and backing layers, and smooth out again.

Keeping the layers smooth at all times, pin- or hand-baste the quilt in a grid pattern starting from the center, working towards the edges at 4" intervals for hand or machine quilting. If your quilt will be machine-quilted by a professional machine quilter, do not baste the layers together. Allow an extra 3"–4" all the way around your quilt top with your backing and batting. Please refer to your own machine quilter's requirements.

Quilt as desired or follow the photograph to mimic what we have done. A motif was placed into each corner of the center block and then all backgrounds were filled with a McTavishing design. You could use any favorite filler here, but try not to take the spotlight away from the Colourquéd Baltimore designs with extravagant quilting.

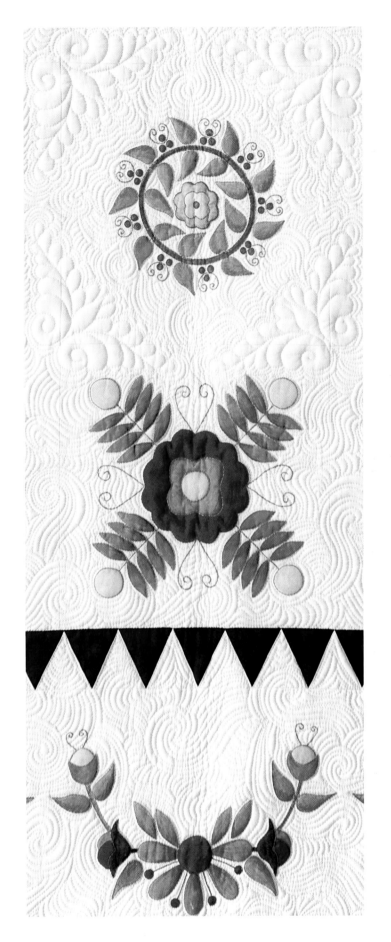

Binding

Join the 6 strips of 2½" wide red binding fabric together using a 45° angle.

Press the long strip in half with the wrong sides together. Align the raw edge of the binding to the raw edge of the quilt and sew with a ¼" seam, mitering the corners as you go. You want to be stitching accurately here so that you get perfect points on your outside pieced borders. Trim the excess from the edges of the batting and backing to ½" from the seam line and turn the binding to the back.

To finish the quilt, slip stitch the binding to the back with a thread that matches the binding fabric.

Tip:

If you attach the label before the quilting step, it will be quilted to the quilt and very difficult for another "lover" of your quilt to remove.

Hanging sleeve

If your quilt is going in a competition, exhibition, or just going to be hung in your home, it is a good idea to attach a hanging sleeve as you attach your binding. See page 15 on hanging sleeve instructions if you wish to do this.

Labelling

Last, but most important, is to make a label for your quilt that includes your name, address, the date, the name of the quilt, and any other relevant details. The best thing to use is a permanent pen to ensure the details don't wash away. Or, you may wish to make a Colourquéd label using a design feature from the front and embroider or pen stitch the writing with a permanent pen. Stitch this to your quilt so that future generations will know the creator!

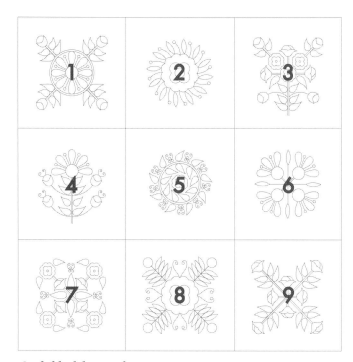

Quilt block layout diagram

Faux Appliqué — Helen Stubbings

Colourqué block 1

reduce block 60% for
MINI BALTIMORE quilt

Colourqué block 2

reduce block 60% for
MINI BALTIMORE quilt

Faux Appliqué — Helen Stubbings

Colourqué block 3

reduce block 60% for
Mini Baltimore quilt

BLESSED BALTIMORE

Colourqué block 4

reduce block 60% for
MINI BALTIMORE quilt

Faux Appliqué — Helen Stubbings

Colourqué block 5

reduce block 60% for
MINI BALTIMORE quilt

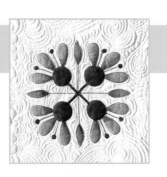

Colourqué block 6

reduce block 60% for
MINI BALTIMORE quilt

Faux Appliqué — Helen Stubbings

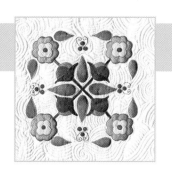

Colourqué block 7

reduce block 60% for
MINI BALTIMORE quilt

BLESSED BALTIMORE

Colourqué block 8
reduce block 60% for
MINI BALTIMORE quilt

Faux Appliqué — Helen Stubbings

Colourqué block 9
reduce block 60% for
MINI BALTIMORE quilt

Colourqué pattern–border

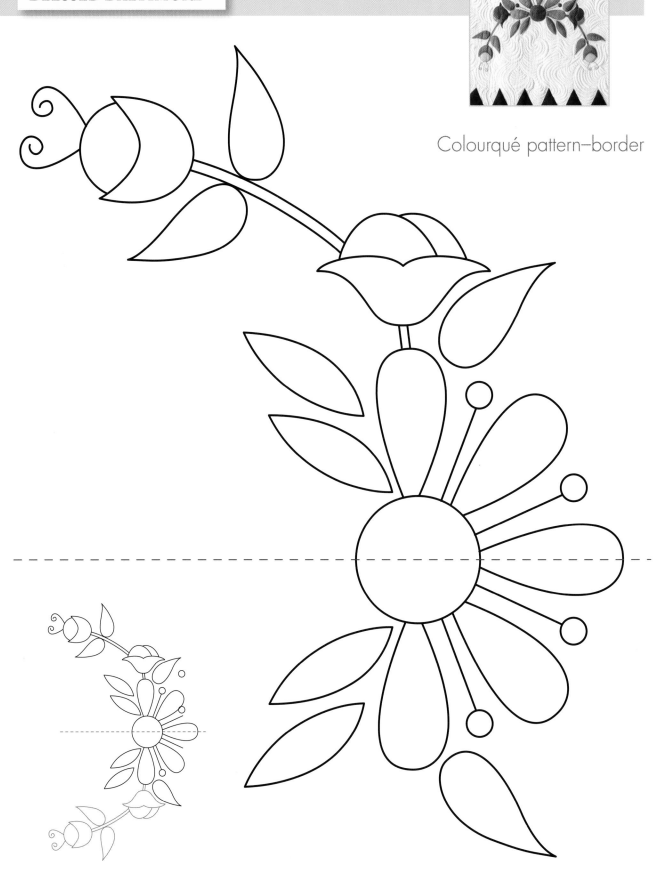

Faux Appliqué — Helen Stubbings

Colourqué pattern—border corner

Foundation Templates

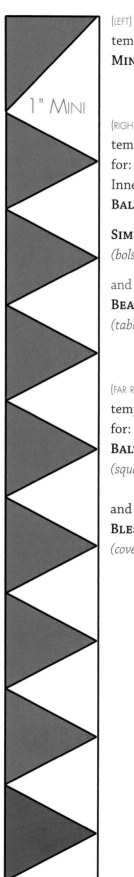

1" MINI

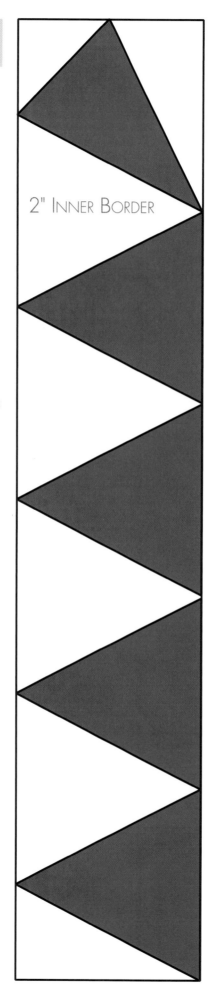

2" INNER BORDER

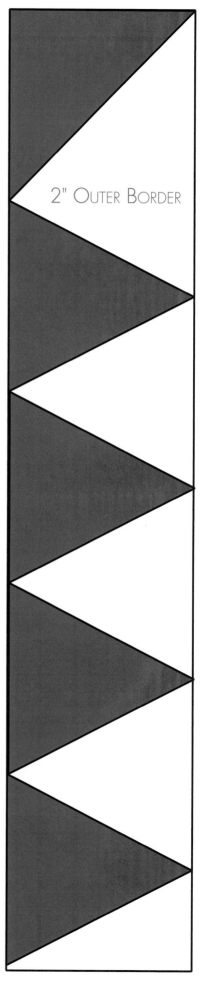

2" OUTER BORDER

(LEFT) 1" foundation template for:
MINI QUILT

(RIGHT) 2" foundation template inner border for:
Inner border **BLESSED BALTIMORE** *(cover quilt)*

SIMPLY BALTIMORE *(bolster cushion)*

and

BEAUTIFUL BALTIMORE *(table runner)*

(FAR RIGHT) 2" foundation template outer border for:
BALTIMORE BOUNTY *(square pillow)*

and outer borders for **BLESSED BALTIMORE** *(cover quilt)*

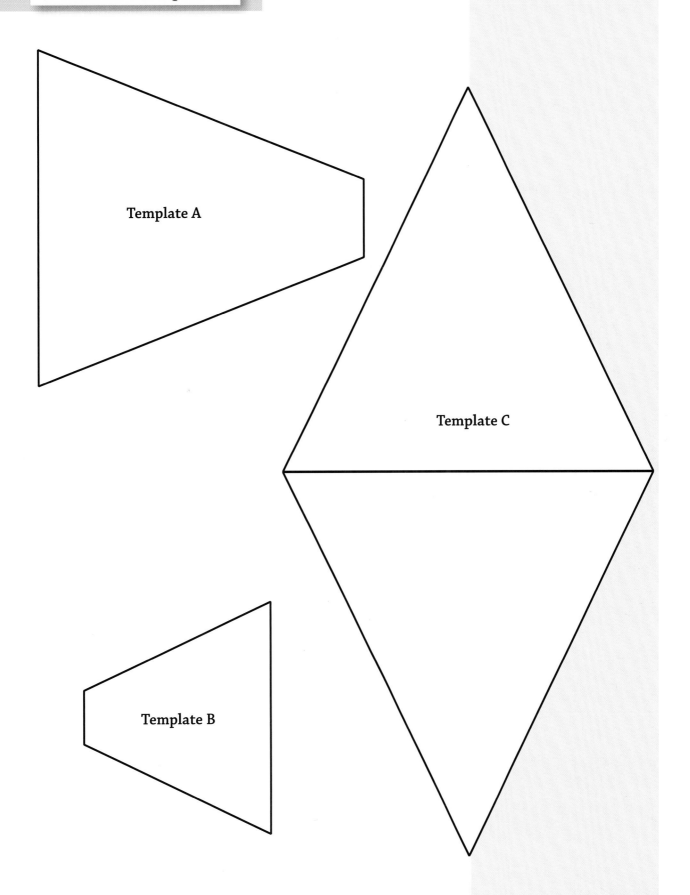

Template A

Template C

Template B

Taking Colourqué One Step Further

Faux Appliqué — Helen Stubbings

There are many other variations and extensions of the basic Colourqué technique which will be saved for another book. However, here is a glimpse of some effects you can get and some different variations of Colourqué in my Gallery.

(OPPOSITE) DAISY DANCE

54" x 54". Made by the author, quilted by Tracey Browning.

This quilt used the traditional color, seal, and stitch method. It had to be done in this order because the soft pink color being so soft would have disappeared during the stitching process if not sealed first. Derwent Studio pencils were used for the coloring. The whole quilt took two pencils of each color to complete.

Medallion-style quilts can combine appliqué, piecing, and Colourqué quite stunningly. Compare the Colourqué version of DAISY DANCE with the appliqué version! PHOTO: © RICHARD BARREN

(RIGHT) AURORA STUBALIS

10" x 14½". Made by the author.

This was a quick quilt made for a local challenge using the new Derwent Inktense range of pencils. When water is added they give a wonderful ink-like translucent effect. Blending is easy, and although they are said to be permanent once water has been added, I sealed with textile medium instead of water to ensure this. I added beading and played with some free-motion machine quilting ideas to complete the small letter-size quilt.

PHOTO: HELEN STUBBINGS

Faux Appliqué — Helen Stubbings

LACE #2, *58" x 58".*

Colourquéd by the author, quilted by Tracey Browning.

This quilt was designed and completely finished as a wholecloth quilt by Tracey Browning on a long-arm machine. It was then Colour-quéd by myself, taking approximate-ly 80–100 hours to color. But imag-ine how many hours it would have taken to needle-turn appliqué it? I used Coloursoft pencils and used the medium to blend my colors and move the color to the edges of the quilted and trapuntoed sections.

PHOTO: CHARLES R. LYNCH

VICTORIAN VIRTUOSO, *37" x 42". Made by the author.*

The design for this quilt was inspired by a glass etching and was in-tended as a wholecloth design. I transferred the design onto my fabric and colored and sealed using two shades of a blue Derwent Coloursoft pencil. These pencils are very soft and act similarly to a watercolor.

When sealing with textile medium I was able to move the color around and blend my two colors smoothly. The top was then layered and hand basted before the outlines were free-motion machine outline quilted in a matching blue Aurifil thread. The background was quilted using a cream Superior MasterPiece™ thread. Hot-fix Swarovski® crystals were added for extra effect and design detail. Monotone color always has a fantastic WOW impact, don't you think?

PHOTO: HELEN STUBBINGS

Faux Appliqué — Helen Stubbings

(ABOVE) CONSTANTINE FARM, *86" x 86". Made by the author, quilted by Tracey Browning.*

A single black thread has been used as an outline element in CONSTANTINE FARM *to give it a cartoonish, coloring book look. It could be easily "stitched" with black Pigma® pen, or if using a screen-printed kit, just left with the black screen-printed ink only.* PHOTO: © RICHARD BARREN

(OPPOSITE, TOP) FAIRY KISSES, *78" x 78". Made by the author, quilted by Tracey Browning.*

In this quilt I used the color, stitch, and then seal method. I colored quite darkly and used lots of blending. Stitching first took away a lot of the intensity of color and also blended my colors smoothly before sealing. Pencils used were from the Derwent Studio range. PHOTO: © RICHARD BARREN

(OPPOSITE, BOTTOM) FAIRY FLOSS, *58" x 72". Made and quilted by the author.*

Colourqué replaces appliquéd vines in this quilt. PHOTO: © RICHARD BARREN

Resources

PFD fabric – prepared for dying fabric
US – *Available from many fabric distributors and local quilting stores*
Australia – *PFD T500 – 114 optical white stitchery fabric* Victorian Textiles p:03 95551115
e:info@victoriantextiles.com.au

Red fabric used in all projects
Shadow Play Style 513 Colour R14
US – Maywood Studio **www.maywoodstudio.com**
Australia – Lloyd Curzon textiles.
http://www.lcurzon.com.au/craft.htm

Pencils – Derwent Artist pencils
Made by the Cumberland Pencil Company UK
http://www.pencils.co.uk
World wide store locater: **http://www. winsornewton.com/retailers/globalsearch.html**

Textile Medium™ – Folk Art brand by Plaid
http://www.plaidonline.com/   800-842-4196

Freezer paper:
US – *Reynolds Freezer paper is available in your supermarkets or quilting stores.*
Australia – *available in quilting stores.*

Presencia Threads Finca Perle #16
http://www.presenciausa.com/
Australia – Distributed by Ristal Threads
http://www.ristalthreads.com/
e:info@ristalthreads.com   P:02 62412261

DMC conversion:
    Presencia 1996 = DMC 221
    Presencia 4561 = DMC 987
    Presencia 5229 = DMC 3012
    Presencia 2240 = DMC 3687

DMC threads
Worldwide store locator at **http://www.dmc-usa. com/majic/pageServer/0h01000057/en_US/ Store-search.html**

Piping Hot Binding and Groovin' Piping trimming tool (Kit includes book and tool) – Susan Cleveland **www.piecesbewithyou.com**
e-mail: **PiecesBeWithYou@worldnet.att.net**

Constantine Quilts – Tracey Browning
tracey@constantinequilts.com
www.constantinequilts.com

Hugs 'n Kisses patterns
www.hugsnkisses.net
email **helen@hugsnkisses.net**

About the Author

Helen lives with her three daughters and husband in Tasmania, Australia's island- and southern-most state.

She runs her two businesses, Hugs 'n Kisses and Wysistas— maker of Quizzles®, interactive quilt patterns— from her home studio producing patterns, books, and CDs for the textile, stitching, quilting, home decorating, and craft industries. Her projects have appeared in many Australian and U.S. magazines, and she has exhibited and been awarded many honors for her quilts worldwide.

Helen has taught her Colourqué® technique throughout Australia and internationally for several years and particularly loves the gathering/retreat type setting where women come together and share in the joy of stitching.

She also volunteers her time to several charity projects such as "Snugglybug Rugs" and runs charity friendship days in her local area.

Helen can be contacted at:
email: helen@hugsnkisses.net
PO Box 390
Lenah Valley Tasmania 7008 Australia
+61 362787507
Or view her Web sites at:
www.hugsnkisses.net
www.wysistas.com
www.patternpress.com.au – *wholesale e-commerce site*